Unraveled Soul

Free verse poetry

Kaitlin Wendell

BookLeaf
Publishing

India | USA | UK

Presentation by *BookLeaf Publishing*

Web: www.bookleafpub.com

E-mail: info@bookleafpub.com

ISBN: 9789363312135

First edition 2024

This book is dedicated to my parents. Without their support throughout my whole journey as a writer; this couldn't be possible.

Acquitted Love

Hard to forget
The love I left behind
With thoughts of regret
Anything new will be declined
All the past hurt swelling up inside
A set back redefined
Never ending struggle of throwing away the good
A love so misunderstood
Yet here I dwell in the chaos of it
An understanding I am acquit
It's apart of me now
An unwritten vow
The past is a ghost within me
I am married to its memory

Shackled

Shackled to the false love
Holding on to the lie
Hoping its not true
Yet here i am disposed of
The heartache, i can't deny
If only the better i knew
I wouldn't be stuck in my own demise
Listening to my burning cries

War of the Bottle

Staring at this bottle as if it will stop me from going insane
Again...I apologize to my heart and brain
This whole thing is killing me inside
Yet, I keep telling my demons I will abide
I guess I am addicted to the sin
My eternal demons always win
They are laughing at my pain
I'm held captive in their domain
Beating me till I can't fight anymore
I become a prisoner of their war
Wanting to escape this agony
However, I keep putting myself through the animosity
This bottle has ran dry
Regret has set in making me cry.

The End of Life's Quest

Listening to the soft beats of the heart
Thinking my life needs a restart
Feeling like I never measured up
In need of a major glow up
My ducks are not in a row
Definitely have some room to grow
Yet I sit here not trying
My mind is just crying
No motivation to keep going
The end result is already showing
I have truly failed
Success has set sailed
Power of darkness took control
I lie empty in my soul
My life has been laid to rest
Nothing more on this quest

Risqué Trauma

Living life in sin
Thoughts in a tailspin
The harlot past had awakened
From the trauma it's been shakened
The damage done to her
Caused an eternal massacre
She can never go back before it all started
The old her has surely departed
Ripped from her roots
On a journey of risqué pursuits
Rue the day that ruined her
With sex, drugs, and liquor
Her innocent soul faded away
Carnal urges led her astray
She becomes her trauma
Bested by all the karma

Lonely Ignorant Love

Meantly not prepared for what's to come
All this pain and heartache, I just want to be done
Don't know if I have the strength to keep going
So much for already knowing
Everyday I lie awake, hoping things were different
But I guess that it's just my heart being ignorant
True love and I don't mix well
Doomed for chaos and hell
Yet I keep trying
To find a love so satisfying
Always leaving me empty-handed
Alone and stranded

Love Intervention

In a constant struggle to breathe
All the love I crave always leaves
Can't help to feel like I am worthless
Exploding from all this mess
The harlot past coming up from its grave
To speak revenge on its bitter slave
People tell me not to go back to my old ways
But at least I wasn't lonely all my days
I guess I am in a little desperation
In need of a love intervention

Fake Love Pain

Choking from the pain and heartache
In constant struggle feeling all love is just fake
When all seems to be perfect
At any moment all could be wrecked
A bomb blows up in my face
A piece of my heart is eraced
I don't know how much more I can take
Don't know if I can handle more heartbreak
The future I cannot predict
But much more pain is bound to afflict
Blocking out every embrace
So all this fake love cannot deface

TIME TO SURVIVE

my body in a trance
Thoughts in a spiral dance
Trapped in this fictional glass case
My sin erupting in my face
Drowning from the demons of the past
All my regret on broadcast
Transparent to the devils of this planet
Feeling like I am just in a place of stagnant
My eternal flame ignites
My inner beast ready to fight
I am busting out of this dark place
No longer feeling like I am a disgrace
I am finally free and alive
It's time to SURVIVE

Let Us Be

With hatred in your soul
And heart full of black coal
You suck the joy right out
And fill the room with doubt
Dealing with you is an all out war .
cause you are all about yourself and nothing
more
You lie to make yourself look good
And don't do anything you should
Refusing to be an adult
Will always bring you a negative result
Causing an emotional prison
Because you don't want to listen
Get out of our life
We don't need any more strife
We just want to be happy
So just let us be…..

Pleasure of Love

Deep in the shadows
A voice that bellows
Hidden in secrecy
The spirit of indecency
Filled with naughty flavor
The art of the player
Born out of lust
The golden pleasure is a must
The body craving a touch
Your soft lips coming in a clutch
Our souls aligned
Our hearts intertwined
Fireworks of love in the sky
As pain and heartache say goodbye

My Number One

Addicted to the pleasure
The warmth of his embrace
Finding this love is such a treasure
The constant need to be in this place
When he looks into my eyes
All my sadness slowly dies
The Glow of his smile lights up a room
His love for me in full bloom
Just knowing he's there makes my anxiety
disappear
He's like a warm cup of coffee
Living with no fear
So Smooth and elegant against my body
He's my number one catch
A perfect match

Killer Weapon

My mind filled with expectation
Yet my heart is in a desperation
Linking up for the eternal gain
But only running into empty pain
Angry thoughts of being alone
Turn the golden love I have into stone
Watch out for now I am a weapon
On a journey to teach you a lesson
My lips become the gun, my smile the trigger
My kisses are the bullets, I am your killer.

The Grave of Abusive Love

My heart is guarded with my back against a wall
Don't want to be hurt, don't want to fall
I guess I am used the heartache
The drunken nights and abusive fights
Sending my mind and soul into a sizzere shake
Always feeling like i am not good enough
The road to happiness always seems so rough
Yet here i am humbled by the whole experience
Wondering about my own true existence
Will I ever see the love i crave
Or am i just someone's body slave
Broken down and heated.
Cheated and defeated
Laying in the grave dug for me
Lost, silent, bleeding and ready to flee
Yet trapped by the chaos that consumed me
I am the ghost of this decree

Harlot Reality

Falling weak to the temptation
Addicted to the sensation
Dreaming of a lovely imagination
But only receiving a harlot fabrication
Trying so hard to measure up
Yet always leaving tired and burnt up
I guess I am just a hookup
Even though I have a lot of good in my makeup
Looks like forever alone
Doing everything on my own
Yet i want love to be shown
And that I actually wanted to be known.

A Mark Left Behind

He was the demon in which she can't escape
Sewn together the souls begin their reshape
Bounded to the shadows of the hells they have endured
Fighting for a chance to feel secured
With blood on their hands
And agony in their hearts
Their love for each other departs
Can't forget their story post
Leaving behind the memories of their ghosts
A legend in which they host

Colliding souls

The spirit of the soul
Collides with the energy within the heart
Creating a pathway into the imagination black
hole
Giving us the power from the start
To stand up in the darkness and freely taking
control of our own freedoms
Living in the vastness
Bleeding from past demons
We become the beacons of our own destiny
Trotting through the universe of space and time
Effortlessly giving off our inner ecstasy
Intertwining with the spirits who came before us
in the meantime
We lay to rest the shadows of ourselves
In the star dust within our cells
Silence in the soul as the spirits take control.

Toxic War

Brittled by inauthenticity
Breathing in a toxicity
Trapped by the cage of vulgarity
Living in peace is such a rarity
Rumors and lies clouding the brain
Believing the thoughts with such disdain
Lashing out against the innocent
Making it seem like they are deviant
The war has just begun
The power is not in the gun
It lies within the heart of the victim
The battle will be won
Cause Karma will have the deed be done.

LOVE LOST

Smiling to hide the pain
But deep inside I am going insane
Feeling my soul get ripped apart
Every time you give someone else your heart
Longing for your love and affection
But left with the ideas of rejection
Thinking why am I not what you want?
Why am I put behind this front?
I try to be your everything
Yet I never measure up to every new being
I just want to be loved and appreciated
Not left in the dust and hated
I guess I am not good enough for you
Story of my life it's true
I am never your number one
It definitely hurts a ton
Just have to face the fact
My life and who I am doesn't attract
Loving someone who doesn't love you the same
way
Just burns your soul and heart away

Doesn't cost a thing to pay attention.

Pay attention to the details of life
Read between the lines of its conflict
Doesn't cost a thing to understand the meaning
of the strife
To know the battles of the addict
The constant struggle for the real
But all you get is the fake persona of it
Supposed to have love and support in your feels
Blood thicker than water becomes unfit
Leave the drama and past behind
Don't look back at the demons that once
controlled
Life is better on the other side you will find
Your future is the joy to behold
With God nothing can stop the success
Ride that roller coaster all night and day long
Let the relationships confess
What is right is right and what is wrong is
wrong.
Live, laugh, love is the model intention
Doesn't cost a thing to pay attention

You are blessed

Life is filled with ups and downs
Heartache...drama the things meant to break our crown
But God gives us the tools to conquer
Becoming glow sticks, when we break we shine and prosper
Trials and tribulations make us stronger to face the strongholds of life
It may seem like a lot of strife
Meant to tear us apart
But God has your back from the start
Just believe in yourself and God will take care of the rest
Remind yourself you are blessed.

Love breaks Strongholds

Past pain haunting present happiness
Shutting out community;creating a mess
Preventing success of future goals
Corrupting once innocent souls
The ashes of burnt up thoughts dwell within
Soothing the monster of its sin
Fear captivating whoever stands in the wake
The body consuming all of the heartache
Amongst all the eternal carnage
Lies the host to cleanup the garbage
A light in the darkness
An angel with finesse
Stepping out of comfort patrol
And stepping into heavenly control
Love makes a break in
Healing the mind for the win.

Good soul bad intentions

Diverging into unknown existence
Erasing the mere hope of innocence
Yet here I lie in the wasteland of my debravity
Taking part in the utter fantasy
Shedding some light to the depths of the brain
My thoughts making me insane
Scratching at the surface begging to be released
The soul hungry crying for a feast
Yet not even a crumb from the past can save the
heartache
It's about to break
Basking in the puddles of misfortune
Operating in such distortion
However the pureness is not on the outside
It lies within where good and evil collide
The war between the two abide
Making one whole being satisfied.

Journey to love

Brittled by the pain of undesired devotion
Sacrificed by the void of lust emotion
Dragging the heart through utter erosion
Emptiness dwelling inside
Despair and disbelief in my stride
But picking up, moving forward swallow my pride
Here lies the death of me
The future holds the key
To be born again of this degree
Rising from the dust
Healing from all the disgust
My time to shine and adjust
This is my life my victory win
Time to go back to where it all started to begin
Deep in the bellows of within
Beat the damned cracked veil
To summit and not derail
On the path to freedom set to sail
 Into the abyss of the unknown
But I am safe... I AM NOT ALONE.

Battles of the mind

Rising friction
Burning affliction
Craving conviction
Mind obliteration
Heart adoration ...
Soul isolation
Body in diselation
Wanting correction
Getting objection
Having imperfection
Life misconnection
Thought reflection
Dream infection
Devoted injection
Beloved satisfaction

The raw you

Barren Wasteland
Embalming quicksand
Can't escape
This mind-filled rape
My body hate...
Guard the gate
Just see the raw
Apparent dull
Seeking the call
Render Cold
Fixing the mold
Truth awaits
it uncertain dates
Amidst the broken
Heart of its token
This is why
My soul must fly
For it remains deep and dry.

World is not a friend

When the world tries to give you hell
And it seems like you can't do anything right
You just sit there and swell
As your mind goes into a fight
You have no idea what is wrong
The battle will be very long ...
Your soul begins to crumble
As your heart realizes the fumble
You try to walk away from the pain
But all it is making you go is insane
You toss and turn like it's the end of the life
As your body fills up with so much strife
You lay there to rest your head
Since its about to explode across the bed
After a night of constant struggle
You realize all you do is stumble
With or without the support of others
Even without faith from fathers and mothers
You just want to be happy
No matter the cost or the snappy
You want to do your own thing
Because it would mean everything
To live your own life as you see true

Doing what you want to do
You are your own person
Living out the life you always wanted
Your soul beginning it's resurrection
You being you, that is all that needs to be said

My love

You are the thought that breaks my silence,
You are my true uttering reliance
You are everything I ever needed
With you I never feel defeated.
You are my.comforting savior ...
My odds may not be in my favor
However, you are my guiding flavor.
You mean The world to me,
I hope you can see my yearning,
For US to once again be a we.
The love I have for.you is.burning,
Through the fires of my heart
Each morning you are the start.
Each night.you are the end
I want you again and again.

High on life

In the depths of this land I live
I must not keep for so God I give
The realm in the darkness I lay
In the waters of tempting fascination I'll pay
For the alluring nature drives me insane
Body quaking,filling the drain
I must be in on high my mind so fly
Ripping apart the volcanoes or high voyage
Crying out in pure molten foliage
I seek a more scenic route
For now my body lay here in shrout
Uttering satisfaction I bleed
All the time, this I need

Lust

Behind every nook and cranny
Atmosphere all fine and dandy
Submissive to an electric frequency
Connecting rhythmic movements in secrecy
Gentle yet invigorating adrenaline
Igniting the beast within the fantasy medicine
The jowls of the finish line
So lovely and Devine
Birth the cataclysmic ending howl
Not today or tomorrow
A love utter most fowl

Gluttony

Empty cauldron brews
Devouring the witch insoos
Shoveling the cave to toil and trouble
Ready to burst all this mumble jumble
Gobbling up this innocent machine
Cracking open the eager craving scene
Fly west fly east
Oh please lynch this feast.

Wrath

Boiling overtime madness
Danger within us
Irritation rising up to the surface
My heart in a disturbance
Regrets are being resurfaced
My mind on a purpose
Violence ever so earnest
Blood so hot like a furnace
Revenge in the practice
Enemy ready to vanish
 My sworn duty…..so savage

Greed

Longing for indulgence
Seeking the creed of my divulgence
Desire for the fortune
The funds of absorption
Resources in my reach
Materials I need, I beseech
My one and only plea
Give me what I want or flee
My wealth my riches
The treasure within my stitches

Pride

The gratification of the ability
Egotistical nobility
Servitude to the satisfaction
Of one's attraction….reflection
Freedom with some dignity
My results so brilliantly
Rise up in Chivalry
My mind and soul filled with vanity
This I say is humanity
Hashing the honor of fulfilment
Today I am resilient.

Sloth

Drifting into deep slumber
Boredness in high numbers
Laying silent without a force
Inactivity taking its course
Pondering life without living it
Working is so unfit
Lazy makes me truly lit
Doing something today very unlikely
Slacking off my point exactly
Lay back and watch time go by
Relax my friend, I am satisfied.

Envy

Rising up In Jealousy
Covet thy neighbor so heavily
Craving what I don't poses
Creates such an angry mess
The desire to be just like everyone
Even though I don't hold the key to the fun
I long for the win, I must conquer
Give me your everything
I want to be the one true king.

Haunting Past

38

As I lay dying
whispers of a harsh reality burst forth
Ridged cracks of the past diverge
Flashes of life try to intervene henceforth
My eyes burn with ashes, pain will emerge
Thoughts fade in fear
My breathing in defiance
Shadows of the brain seen the atmosphere
My body lies cold, the air is still….silence.

Dreams.

Death is never dead
Even though it is full of dread
It's just the beginning
Endless realm in Hiding
Fantasy land of forgotten folklore
Mystical wonders fill the core
Magical moments fly through the sky
 The freeness hard to come by
Silent secrets hold the key
To the beauty within the grave mystery
Untouched catacombs of revelations
Daunting chariots drive the luxury sensations
Arriving at the oasis of the kingdom
Gaining the body of wisdom

Sex

The inner crevice swells with intensity
Body fills with ecstasy
Inner walls crave attention immensely
A touch ever so gently
Makes the lining cave in a frenzy
Felt amazing in a plenty
Inside is where the party at
Sliding in and out is the format
Positioning in full throttle combat
This the one true habitat
Where I want to be becoming so free

War on earthly demons

Combat with the demons within
Just to live an honorable legacy
Yet what's good in this world leaves you dry and thin
Too nice for my own well being
But a higher power led me to be
However, all i feel is that i should be fleeing
Guarding my heart from earthly cysts
Though my failures always breaking through the mist
How can i possibly enter the peaceful kingdom
If the mind can't shake into freedom
Constant battles to be heard
Sitting in silence is just absurd
 No one wants to listen
They all believe helping must be treason

Saved Dying Life

The clouds have faded to gray
I can't seem to find my way
There is no way out, I want to scream and shout
Please someone help me, I'm dying in this place
My life and death are face to face
I'm self destructing, my life is combusting
Then along came the answer to my prayers
Someone who cares
Along came someone who changed my life
Now I don't need to strive
I saw my life be made anew
Now I knew what to do
The clouds are back to white
I know knew what was right
I can finally live a life of satisfaction without the
misrepresentation
I can live life with certain gratitude without the
false attitude
My life is back on track
No more of an evil attack
No more striving, no more dying
I am a fresh new being
A girl worth seeing
With a life worth believing.

My Box

All my life I've been guarded
It seems like I'm shy targeted
I've been stuck in this box
Complete with many locks
Afraid to come out
Afraid to scream and shout
I was afraid to speak
Afraid of being called weak
I like my box it's quite cozy
But that part of my life is phony
I need to step out and speak my mind
Now is the time
Can't be afraid to speak anymore
Got to shut the fear behind the door
My box has no room for me
It's not where I want to be
Goodbye box you have been cool
But no longer will I be a shy fool

Marching Into Destiny

The journey is rough.
Future may not be so clear.
Everything seems tough.

But I hold so dear,
The very dreams in my head,
Even though I fear,

The unknown ahead.
Knowing the success I bare,
But I think life's dead.

I try not to stare.
Watching people reject me,
It just gives me stress.

Finding who I am.
Marching into Destiny,
Destroying the sham.

Keeping dreams in thee,
Journal of my changing life.
becoming so free,

Running out strife.
Transforming my Destiny.
Accept the new me.

The Beauty Within

It's hard to understand that this person is truly
me.
I see this person every minute,
but don't know who she really is.
The thought just blows me away,
It's like the glimpse of a harvest moon.

I look beyond the point of direction.
To see if I can unveil the future inside,
but what flashes before my eyes is nothing but,
A beast in camouflage.

I have no courage,
no passion, no yearning
It is dreadful to look at,
the person that is me.
But I couldn't look away;
couldn't stop the mutiny of an eclipse.
I have the desire,
but it exploded into a blaze.
My life has turned around,
Around the center of a serene reflection.
The demons within my spirit,

Became atoms of a Black Hole.
Ripping apart the core of my heart,
They shatter what I think is me.

I now have the insight of a new reality,
at which I became a new person.
I look at myself from within,
I am no longer engulfed by foul poison.
The vicious monster inside is fading away,
I am now glowing with the essence of jewels.
I now love and accept this person as me.

A grave Experience

Living yet breathless
Heart beating yet silent
Submitting yet defiant
Yielding yet endless
Unheard, unseen, untouched
The mysteries of the shadows
The forgotten folklore
The air is still…...silence
Like a grave; unconscious
Yet burning for madness
A heartbeat rises from the ashes
The carcuses ignite the witches
The wicked slaughter the truth
They gobble up the once innocent town
It's time for the lynching
The spirit lies cold
As if this were all a dream.

The battles to be Free

Heart racing yet quiet
The trials of the mind defiant
The intimacy in which you see
The battles to be free
The beast within
The evil twin
Ripping apart the core
I never asked for this,
I didn't want more
I never knew the risk
The shadows are caving in
My thoughts are in a spin
Bending yet sustaining
Repair and remove
Accept yet disprove
Fighting and winning

Patriotic Warfare

A flash before my eyes,
a beast in disguise
The American battle cry
rains over the land.
We are alive.
From dusk to dawn
we will go fight,
Even though we fear
the unknown site.
We are the breathless
Laying our hands on the trigger
For the killer; is among us.
The forbidden shadows
slaughter the truth
The burial grounds of the Youth.
Our hearts beating, yet silent
This journey became violent.
But we will sustain; We are free.
Our spirits triumph over Victory!
We are one Blood
We are one.... America!

ARS POETICA

Poetry is the art of the written word,
being shaken and stirred
becoming freely emerged
through endless splurge.

Poetry is the awkward nerd
the transformed absurd,
where the mute are not unheard
but whirred to another herd.

Poetry is the written language of the heart,
creating an image through inscribed art,
so elegantly smart, so lovely at the start,
never wanting to be apart.

Poetry is the imagination of the mind,
intertwined with graceful design,
shielded from world malign.
It is the meaning redefined.

Poetry is a key to intimacy
Into people you will see,

the true calling of their destiny.
It is the written plea to be free.

poetry is the never ending glee,
with fresh decree
molding for future foresee,
it's the American battle key.

9/11

We become one blood,
As pieces of steel and glass flood the streets,
We became one identity,
As heroes help those who can't help themselves,
We became one age,
As we set fire to mourn the unforgotten,
We became one tribe,
As Heroes fight the fire of burning memories,
We become one truth
As we pray for those families who are lost or broken,
We become one life,
As we shout to remember,
We became one mind,
As we fight to to live freely ,
We became one system,
As we sacrifice our own lives for others,
We became one spirit,
As we mourn the people that gave their lives,
We become one America,
As we tell the memories of that day.

Love

A reality in which we crave
Bit into a bitter grave
From lost to save
We live to be
Yet, never get thee
In which we see
The realness of it
Corrosion of the pit
Became so lit
The end so caustic
It seems like a diagnostic
Progressing to the next
The journey so complex
Energy mirror reflects
Dawn to thee rejects
For see thy pal
Level up my morale.

Restoring Me

Shadows creeping in
Face to face with my sin
Here I am in the flesh
Surrounded in this mesh
I can't see me ...
Who I am supposed to be
Darkness sets amid
Enemies take a bid
My soul takes some heat
As my mind creates defeat
My heart, the faster it keeps beating
My body begins its fleeting
In the distance there is a light
A tunnel of great might
Follow till the end
My wounds mend
My scars are fading away
I say to myself, I will be OK
My heart becomes renewed
My soul and mind stop being in a feud
The struggle is released
All battles within will cease
My body laid to rest

I will enjoy life with happiness
My inner lion roared
My life is adored
This is me restored

Beloved Ashes

Fire in my soul, Ashes in my blood,
dark as Coal Shadows thick as mud
Here I am Sitting quietly in my head
The demon in my brain wants to be fed
The dream is so sacred but ripped to a shred. ...
Burning inside the thoughts collide
The light so rare in the chaos
Demon coming alive in the haziness
A light scream leaves my body
Imploding from within so oddly
I am just sitting here
Contemplating my life in fear
My demon looking at me so vivid
Face to face and timid
He breathes animosity into my eyes
Like he knows the pain within my cries.
Connected by choice not by need
My heart becomes the feed
The satisfaction leads to see
The strength of my inner me
The masking is unveiled
True to me set sailed
Above and beyond the possible

The mountains are now conquerable
I am me, I am loved
This is who I am, beloved.

ODE TO WRITING

The way the pen feels in my hand
Is the way writing is meant to understand
The thoughts deep inside
Breaking the thresholds like the tide
The verses running through my head
Freely connecting what is said
Writing is the love I crave
Through characters come alive and heroes save
Transporting to another realm
Where fantasies want to overwhelm
Stories appear before my eyes
Through creatures come to disguise
To think the impossible
To conquer the impending obstacle
The written language of the heart
Creating an image through inscribed art
Remembering the past
Enjoying the present
And foretelling the future
The backgrounds are all but a rumor
The imagination of the story
Translating emotion into inspirational glory
Writing can cuddle like a cloud or slice like a knife
Writing is truly the love of my life.

www.ingramcontent.com/pod-product-compliance
Lightning Source LLC
Chambersburg PA
CBHW061717130726
47996CB00006B/2355